Hello there!

Welcome aboard your Nessie adventure!

NESSIE: A MONSTER KIDS GUIDE! - is your key to unlocking an ancient mystery!

Sharing the history, folklore, evidence, and adventure surrounding the hunt for the Monster of Loch Ness!

It includes postcodes (zip codes) and coordinates of some of the best Nessie hotspots around the Loch, advice on monster hunting equipment, famous sightings and compelling evidence, and the best times and conditions to spot this shy and elusive beast!

Whether you're a first-time visitor, an avid monster hunter, or simply curious about the legend of the Loch Ness Monster, this guide is perfect for you.

Designed to enhance your experience on-site or from the comfort of your own home, it is a versatile companion for all!

Will you be the one to prove that Nessie is REAL!?

Good luck!

A Brief History...

Loch Ness is a freshwater loch in the Scottish Highlands that forms part of the Great Glen, a geological fault which runs from Inverness in the north to Fort William in the south.

It is the largest body of water in the British Isles, holding an astonishing 263 billion cubic feet of water. It is Britain's second deepest body of water, after Loch Morar, plunging to a staggering 755 feet in depth!

Although the Loch Ness Monster may seem to be a modern phenomenon, ancient Scottish folktales tell of a water-dwelling creature known as the Kelpie or Water Horse (Scottish Gaelic: Each-Uisge) that haunted many Scottish lochs but was known to love the deep dark waters of Loch Ness, best!

But is the Loch Ness Monster real? Let's look at some of the highs and lows of Nessie-Hunting over the years and see if we can convince you!

Hunting the Monster

Since the birth of Nessie-mania, many expeditions have been launched by hopeful adventurers who have tried almost everything to capture evidence of the beast. However, this shy and elusive creature has always stayed one step ahead of her would-be capturers!

Fun fact: Over the years, teams of water watchers armed with binoculars, film cameras, telescopic lenses, hydrophones (underwater listening devices), acoustic sonar nets, submersible strobe-lit cameras, diving bells, submarines, ROVs, thermal drones, night vision cameras, eDNA testing, and even a baited cage, have all been deployed to hunt for the Loch Ness Monster!

The Flipper Photo: In 1972, the Academy of Applied Science expedition led by Robert H. Rines claimed to have captured several images of Nessie using sonar and submersible cameras. The most famous of these is "the Flipper Photo", which shows the rhomboid-shaped flipper of a large unknown animal.

So, as you begin your hunt for the Loch Ness Monster, don't be discouraged if you don't manage to snap a photo right away. You may not have a sonar-equipped camera, but who knows, you might capture evidence of a flipper ...or two!

A Prehistoric Stowaway

The creature most commonly associated with the Loch Ness Monster is the plesiosaur, a now-extinct aquatic lizard that lived at the same time as the dinosaurs… but, how could a plesiosaur still be alive today, and are there any known animals that could explain sightings of the Loch Ness Monster?

Monster Imposters: Sceptics around the world have come up with several monster imposter candidates, such as - *Sturgeon, Wels Catfish, Giant Eel, Greenland Shark, Seal, Otter, Swimming Deer, Boat Wakes, Standing Waves, Seismic Gas, Floating Logs*, and even an escaped *Elephant* - to explain sightings of the Loch Ness Monster!

A Prehistoric Stowaway
continued...

Giant Eel: In the past, when eel fishing was more popular, local tales of huge specimens measuring over 10 feet in length were common in loch ness, such as that of the giant eel-like creature found in the Corpach Lock at the other end of the Caledonian Canal in 1900.

Could an eel explain some of the features described in many Nessie-sightings? Happily, no! Eyewitnesses regularly report several physical features that would be impossible for an eel (no matter how big it is) to mimic!

What to look for...

Witnesses describe seeing a large oval hump that resembles an upturned boat or several humps, protruding from the water. Others describe seeing a long neck with a small horse-like or eel-like head gliding through the water. Nessie has also been spotted on land – with several eyewitnesses describing her as having a large oval body, four flippers, a long neck with a small head, and a long, flat tail.

When to look...

Recent statistical analysis of 1,500 recorded Nessie sightings has shown that the best times to see Nessie are on a Saturday or Sunday, at 11 a.m. and 3 p.m., especially when the loch is flat and calm!

S M T W T F S

How to look...

There are many ways to search for Nessie, such as taking a trip on one of the many sonar-equipped cruise boats available around the loch or staking out a popular Nessie hotspot from the shore. A good pair of binoculars and a camera at the ready will help capture proof of this shy and elusive creature.

Where to look...

If you're hoping to spot Nessie, you are spoilt for choice, as she has been seen at Dores, Foyers, Brackla, Drumnadrochit, Abriachan, Invermoriston, Fort Augustus, Urquhart Castle and Urquhart Bay. However, some spots are better than others, with Urquhart Castle and Urquhart Bay being the most popular locations to encounter the beast!

That's it; now you have all the information you need for a successful Nessie sighting. Here are 10 key sighting hotspots to start you off. Good luck on your Nessie hunt!

Remember to mark the places you've been!

☑ I was here _____

☑ I saw Nessie _____

Deepest point of Loch Ness
coordinates: 57.324493, -4.440741

Loch Ness is a freshwater loch in the Scottish Highlands that forms part of the Great Glen, a geological fault that runs from Inverness in the north to Fort William in the south.

It is the largest body of water in the British Isles, holding an astonishing 263 billion cubic feet of water and plunging to a staggering depth of 755 feet!

Fun Fact: George Edwards, the skipper of the "Nessie Hunter" tour boat, claimed to have captured a deeper reading of 812 feet on his fish finder somewhere in the vicinity of Urquhart Castle.

☐ I was here _____

☐ I saw Nessie _____

First sighting

Although there have been more than 1500 sightings of the Loch Ness Monster since the Inverness Courier published an article titled - "Strange Spectacle in Loch Ness" in 1933; the first recorded encounter actually took place in the River Ness in 565AD, when Saint Columba rescued one of his followers from the beast by making the Sign of the Cross and saying, "Go no further. Do not touch the man. Go back at once!"

☐ I was here _____

☐ I saw Nessie _____

Viewing Point on the A82
IV2 6TR

On 15 April 1933, Aldie Mackay and her husband saw an enormous creature with the body of a whale rolling in the water in the loch, while driving along the A82, towards Inverness.

Can you see it? From the viewing point, on the A82, look towards Aldourie, perhaps Nessie might just make an appearance for you!

☐ I was here _____

☐ I saw Nessie _____

Alltsigh Youth Hostel
(formerly Alltsigh Halfway House)
IV63 7YD

The most famous photo: Now believed to be a hoax, the "Surgeon's Photograph" taken by London gynaecologist - Robert Kenneth Wilson in 1934, is probably the most recognisable image of the Loch Ness Monster and depicts what appears to be the monster's head and neck.

Take your own photo (or clip) and become the next (or first) person to capture a genuine photo of Nessie!

☐ I was here _____

☐ I saw Nessie _____

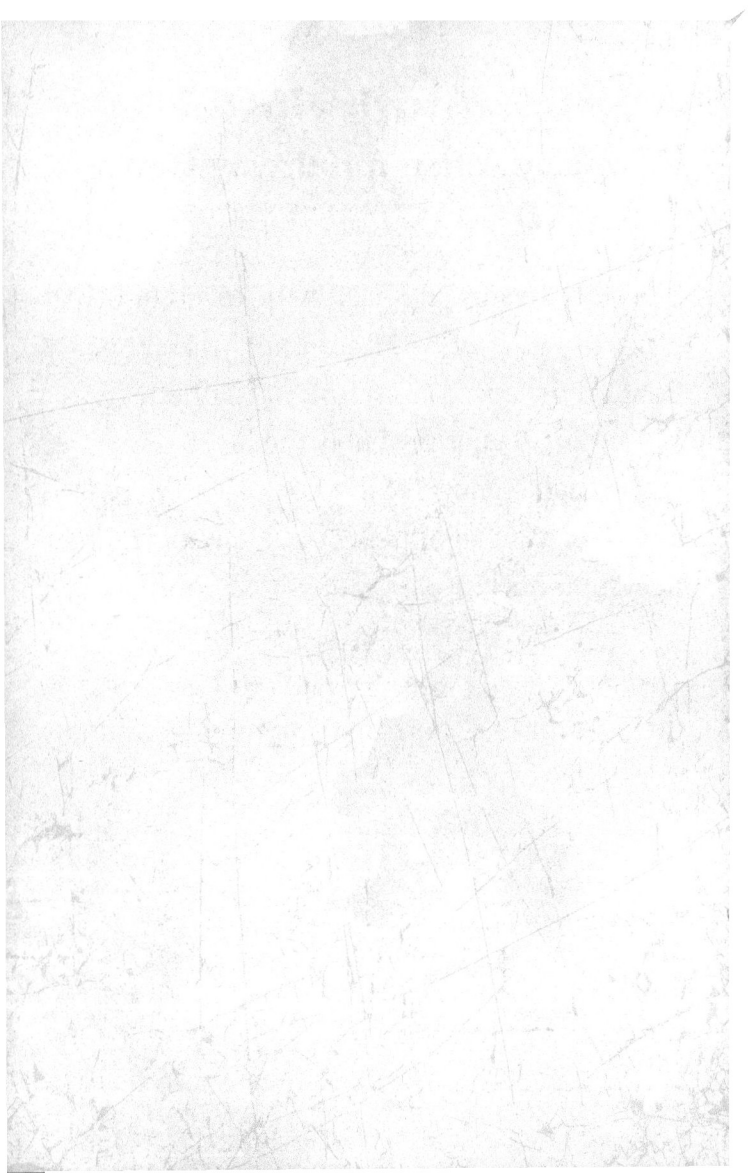

Loch Ness Clansman Hotel
IV3 8AU

On 5 January 1934, veterinary student, Arthur Grant, claimed to have nearly hit the creature with his motorbike, while driving towards Abriachan at about 1 a.m. According to Grant, it had a small head attached to a long neck; the creature saw him, and crossed the road back to the loch.

So, why did Nessie cross the road? Yet another mystery left unanswered...

☐ I was here _____

☐ I saw Nessie _____

Urquhart Castle
IV63 6XJ

On 29th July 1955, Peter MacNab photographed two long, black humps in the water near Urquhart Castle. Over the years, many researchers have critiqued this sighting stating that the humps could easily have been produced by the combined effect of three trawlers travelling closely together up the loch.

Go to Urquhart Castle and see if you can spot Nessie's humps. Don't forget to ask Nessie to smile for your photo!

☐ I was here _____

☐ I saw Nessie _____

Foyers Pier
IV2 6YB

On the 23rd April 1960, Aeronautical engineer Tim Dinsdale filmed a dark hump crossing Loch Ness. The footage caused a new wave of Nessie-mania after experts at the Joint Air Reconnaissance Intelligence Centre confirmed it showed an 'animate object' swimming in the loch.

Will you go viral by snapping a clip of Nessie, the Monster of Loch Ness?

☐ I was here _____

☐ I saw Nessie _____

Loch Ness Lodge
IV3 8AU

In 2014, 6 people saw the Loch Ness Monster from the dining room. This was covered in a number of local and national newspapers.

Fun fact: Author & TV Presenter, Andy McGrath honeymooned at this hotel, 2 years earlier. Sadly, He wasn't one of the 6 fortunate "sight-see-ers".

It is a well-known fact that Nessie doesn't take bookings, but if you're very lucky, THIS could be THE DAY you finally meet her!

☐ I was here _____

☐ I saw Nessie _____

Dores Beach
IV2 6TR

In 2018, Japanese-born translator Chie Kelly snapped 61 photos of the beast from the shores of Dores Beach but hid them for fear of ridicule.

In 2023, she shared them with Veteran Nessie-hunter Steve Feltham, who declared them: "the most exciting photographs ever taken of the Loch Ness Monster!"

Will you snap the next "exciting photograph" of Nessie?

☐ I was here _____

☐ I saw Nessie _____

Fort Augustus South Shore
PH32 4BZ

On August 30th 2023, during the biggest hunt for Nessie in 50 years; free swimmers Matty Wiles & Aga Balinska captured a mysterious 3 humped creature on film while swimming near the south shore in Fort Augustus.

Remember, only the strongest swimmers can take on Loch Ness! But, even if you're one of them, it's best to wear a wetsuit... and don't forget to take your waterproof camera with you!

☐ I was here _____

☐ I saw Nessie _____

Stop and consider...!

Before sharing any evidence you may have captured of the Loch Ness Monster, it's important to make sure it's GENUINE!

I know it's hard to believe, but there have been many hoaxes over the past century.

Surgeon's Photo
Dr Robert Kenneth Wilson, 1934

The Surgeon's Photo, the most famous Nessie-photo, was confirmed as a hoax in 1990.

Although Dr Kenneth Wilson claimed to have taken the photo, it was later revealed to have been organised by Big Game Hunter Marmaduke Weatherell; as revenge against the Daily Mail for exposing an earlier hoax he had created using a hippo foot ashtray!

Nevertheless, this photo is still the most recognisable image of the Loch Ness Monster. It is still regularly featured on postcards, mugs, T-shirts, and newspaper headlines worldwide!

Stuart Humps
Lachlan Stuart, 1951

Stuart claimed to have taken a photo of the Loch Ness Monster's three humps near Urquhart Castle.

In 1984, Richard Frere revealed that Alistair Boyd had shown him (on condition of Frere's silence) the bales of hay that Stuart had photographed.

The top lesson from this hoax is that not all grainy pictures are what they seem to be. AND you cannot trust anyone to keep a secret, especially when it's about Nessie!

Searle Photos
Frank Searle, 1972

Loch Ness investigator Frank Searle was one of the most universally despised researchers to have ever frequented the loch.

Ill-tempered, territorial, and prone to violent outbursts, he was even accused of arson by a rival researcher.

Searle claimed to have captured several compelling Nessie photos, including one which appeared to show the dark body and long neck of a plesiosaur-like creature that was later debunked by the Scottish Sunday Mail in 1976!

The Muppet Photo
Anthony 'Doc' Shiels, 1977

Self-proclaimed Wizard of the West, Surrealist Performer, and Artist - Tony 'Doc' Shiels is probably best known for his comical 1977 photos of the Loch Ness Monster.

Shiels claimed to have captured images of the beast's head and neck cruising through the water while standing at the foot of Urquhart Castle.

Although regularly featured in books and magazines over the years, these pictures, commonly known as 'the Muppet Photos', are considered a poor-quality hoax.

Edward's Hump
George Edwards, 2013

Most Hoaxers take their secrets to the grave... but, on occasion, there are one or two who break the mould, almost gleefully owning up to their success in pranking the gullible masses with their trickery!

One of these is George Edwards, a cruise boat operator who decided to have a little fun with a fibreglass hump that had been leftover from an earlier National Geographic documentary.

Edwards later confessed to the hoax, saying he would happily join the 'Rogues Gallery' of Nessie Hoaxers!

Something to Remember!

This small sample of some of the most famous hoaxes should be a deterrent to any WOULD-BE HOAXERS out there and serve as a reminder that - The TRUTH always COMES OUT in the END!

Personally, I believe there really is an UNKNOWN ANIMAL in Loch Ness and that only GOOD RESEARCH undertaken by Citizen Scientists will lead to its DISCOVERY!

A crucial part of this process is to accurately and objectively record your data...

Field Notes...

Record your findings so you can pinpoint the perfect place to stake out Nessie, the Monster of Loch Ness!

More Field Notes...

Did you remember to log the time and place where you saw her?

Even More Field Notes...

Did you see something unusual? Was there anyone else around? Don't forget to take their contact details to help verify your sighting!

Some More Field Notes...

Help your fellow researchers, record what tools you used to spot the Loch Ness Monster - a camera? a drone? an infra-red laser you launched into space...?

Plans for the Future...

What will you do now that you're an Official
Nessie Researcher? Why not write a blog,
post a vlog, or even create your own Monster
Hunting Manual!

Your Selfie with Nessie

Since ancient times, people have tried to imagine what Nessie looks like. However, to this day, no one has managed to get a genuine close-up photo.

Glue (or draw) your selfie with Nessie below:

About the Author:

Andy McGrath is a paranormal researcher and folklorist with over 25 + years of experience in the field.

He is a Speaker, Investigator, Podcaster (Beastly Theories) and Author (Beasts of Britain/ Hairy Humanoids/ Yeti: A Monster Kids Guide!)

Andy McGrath hosts the television series - Weird Britain, which celebrates the histories, mysteries, folklore and fables of the British Isles!

CAUTION!

NESSIE: A MONSTER KIDS GUIDE! is solely intended to provide an overview of the history, mystery, landscape, and locations surrounding the Nessie legend and should not be used as a trail guide!

Any readers interested in visiting Loch Ness should carefully plan their trip, and, if intending to sail upon its waters, should only hire an experienced skipper from a well-known and reputable provider.

It is also highly recommended that you do not travel alone and always take plenty of provisions, such as food, water, adequate clothing and navigational equipment on any expedition you plan to undertake. The weather in the Scottish Highlands can change quickly, and inexperienced hikers can easily lose their bearings or, at the very least, get a good soaking!

Additionally, many parts of the loch are inaccessible by land, and there more than a few dangerous paths and boggy fens that may look good from the water but often lead to bad ends when travelling on foot!

Remember! *"Hope for the best, but prepare for the worst, and it won't take you by surprise!"*